For Oke

with be...

[signature]

Last Tango with Magritte

Last Tango with Magritte

Lydia Robb

Chapman Publishing

2001

Chapman Publishing
4 Broughton Place
Edinburgh EH1 3RX
Scotland

The publisher acknowledges the award
from the Deric Bolton Trust towards
the publication of this volume.
The publisher acknowledges the financial
assistance of the Scottish Arts Council.

A catalogue record for this volume is
available from the British Library.
ISBN 0-906772-98-2

Chapman New Writing Series
Editor Joy Hendry
ISSN 0953-5306

© Lydia Robb 2001

Lydia Robb is hereby identified as the author of
this work in accordance with Section 77 of the
Copyright, Design and Patents Act 1988.

Cover monoprint by Elizabeth Yule.

All rights are strictly reserved.
Requests to reproduce the text in whole or in part
should be addressed to the publisher.

Some of these poems have appeared in the following magazines and
newspapers: *Chapman, Northlight, Northwords, The Scotsman;*
anthologies: *Caa Doon the Muin, More Scottish Poetry, Present Poets,
Tale Spinners, The West in Her Eye;* competition winner: Scots
Language Society Competitions, Northwords Competition 1997,
Scottish International Poetry Prize 2000.

Printed by
The Bath Press, Bath

Contents

Introduction

Lydia Robb does NOT dye her hair. Her lustrous black hair belies her age. Her poetry too is similarly free from any artificial additions.

She casts a fresh and humane eye on landscapes, geographical and psychological which make the reader pause to examine their own ideas. Her natural poetic voice in both English and Scots has a lyricism that is free from artifice. Her descriptions of the northern vistas resonate with accuracy and penetration, opening up new horizons. She lays unobtrusive little time-bombs that create explosions of delight and appreciation in the reader's mind.

Lydia may need glasses for reading but she has a real poet's vision. She sees the world in a sharp and unsentimental focus but can also take the long view that penetrates to the core of truths big and small at the heart of everyday experience.

There is an almost visceral tug that comes from recognition of such authenticity in poetry. But with Lydia there is also a blast of fresh air to blow through our minds and clear away comfy old perceptions.

As a poet her skill has developed over the years into a mastery of rhythm, metre and syntax – her craft is at her fingertips. In subject matter she has both widened her focus and sharpened her scalpel. The two combined provide a formidable weapon. Look out world this poet may be dangerous!

Jan Natanson

To my three grandchildren;
Mairi, Kirsty and Seumas.

Took off
round loch.
Spied daff
on path.

Round shore,
loads more.
Felt gay
that day.

Gob-smacked
back-tracked,
went home,
wrote poem.

An Augury of Wild Birds

A sharp staccato note announced his coming;
the woodpecker chilled out on the bird-table,
his beak tattooing an omen on the bark.

He sent the sparrows scattering like crumbs
into the darkening October sky.
Two rooks kept their distance in the geans.

Night came with the wild geese lamenting.
Drove upon drove of them, wings creaking like oars,
they set a course across a washed-out moon,

I knew she'd died before the intern spoke;
her stethoscope a wishbone round her neck,
orientated towards clocking out.

I thought of the questions my Mum never asked;
the terrible truths kept under sterile wraps;
the cancer running riot.

He was holding court again this morning,
black cap bobbing like a judge's head.
Then he was off, into a sky erased by rain.

Dolina Making Marmalade

A watered-down January sun
leaks through the
kitchen window.

The ceiling wood
has mellowed
to a maple-syrup brown.

She is standing in
a navy-striped apron,
strings loosening
as she moves.
Stove to sink.
Sink to stove.

Peel curls in thin slivers
from the blade
of her paring knife.

Oranges from Seville.

The air crystallises
with their bitter-sweet smell.

Juices run.
Thick bubbles
somersault
in the jelly-pan.

When the marmalade
is tied down
under shrinking cellophane wraps,
she wipes the dribbles
from the stained glass.

The clock beats in the heart
of this kitchen.

Grey Land

Heidstanes happit wi
crottle broun hunker ahent
the auld kirk-yaird waa.

Hark at the wun's sang
souchin throu the drystane dyke;
a pibroch playin,

a sea maw girnin.
Oot on the machair, spindrift,
spirlin sea-speerits.

This land's made o stane,
scree skellin fae heicht an howe.
Hyne awa haar haps

Canisp an Suilven.
Ayont the brae, bare nakit
banes o coorse breeze-block

ring the new graveyaird.
The bodach shaks his heid, sair
murnin the auld weys.

He turns a deif lug
when Daith comes chappin; he rives
awa the linens.

An omen o craws
heize, bleckened leaves flauchterin
fae winter's branches.

A Race Apairt

A pouderin o snaw – the land ligs lythe
ablow the mune. Yer jewel-bricht sari leuks
at odds. A dwynin rainbow i the mirk,

ye jouk the shaidaes, turn yer ither chowk.
Pent clarts yon stane-faced biggins. BNP,
a neo-nazi emblem, Pakis, blecks

gyne hame. Ye mynd whit sticks and stanes can dae.
Yer fremmit fuit-prents, broukit i the snaw,
a movin pictur, bleck on white. Ye turn

tae a weel-kent soun: the licht's alowe, the glisk
o reid an gowd, the crack o brackin gless.
Yer mither's tuith chaws words she disnae ken.

Ye pick the bitties up an stert again.
The nicht's a sair affront. Ye byde inbye,
syne snib the yett agin the wun o chynge.

West Highland Sabbath

Pale grey vapour
clings to the machair.

Pink-petalled thrift
tilts against the sea breeze.

The smell of peat
permeates the morning.

At the first toll
of the kirk bell
doors open and
men in funereal black
filter from the darkness.

I am clad for summer, yet
my Presbyterian upbringing
leaves me cloaked in guilt.

Aberlemno Revisited

The standing stone is standing under wraps.
The howe is happed in haar. Pale memories
are ghosts, silently mouthing hieroglyphs.

Seal Tribe. Cat Tribe. The Picts have made their mark.
A coiled serpent, a fish, a roosting bird,
symbolic hand-mirror and double disc

describe an other-ness; a burial chamber
cairn or broch. Listen. Can you hear
the murmurings of long-dead ancestors?

Turned on its side, this pitted stone takes on
the outline of a whale, its tracery
dissolving in a smirr of acid rain.

Drowning

I've landed in the deep end of the pool.
Danny Smith is standing on my shoulders.

My life-saving certificates float past
just out of reach. The wording doesn't seem

to hold much water. My lungs fizz till it hurts.
A rope of bubbles spirals from my nose.

A whistle blows. Where has the lifeguard been?
Sorting out his yesterday's affairs.

The woman with the fireside-tartan legs
has swum into his life. His wife has sunk

without trace. I am anchored to the tiles.
This is a joke. Am I to die laughing?

Turning Pages

A young boy opposite in duck-egg blue
shalwar-kameez and navy Nike trainers:

an abandoned *Esquire* in the space between us.
The sharper read for men. First-class sex.

A group of loud-mouthed youths, in tribal gear
appear with bags from Virgin Megastore.

The automatic doors sigh. They move on.
The diesel stops. The station clock ticks back.

Bomb-scarred, dead streets. The war is over,
the platform laid with summer.

A suburban garden. Everything is rosy;
the colour of damsons scattered on bare earth,

rouged cheeks, a wind-filled skirt
holding the shape of her stockinged legs.

Alien names dissolving on my tongue:
Isinglass, Brazil nuts, smoked salmon.

A dream-self stares from a tin-tacked mirror;
memories skewered by a ticket collector.

Momentum gathers up the city:
the glitter of a gold-domed mosque,

derelict factories etched in broken glass,
red-eyed rails, weeds sleeping rough between,

teasel, sorrel, dandelion, cow parsley
and a solitary dog-rose shedding ivory.

Should Auld Acquaintance Be Forgot?

The louvres blur their edges.
The speakers fizz with static.
We've listened to the Old Year
ticking out, the New Year clocking in.

Through the mists of alcohol,
ghosts of my past drift by in
sideburns, mini-skirts and kipper ties.

In the background,
Frank Sinatra is doing it his way.
A familiar figure of speech
raps out an advance warning
in peerie-heels and taffeta
crackling like an onion skin.

She comes with
angostura-bitters on her tongue.
I do believe you've put on weight
she says, tucking my label in (C&A's).
You still married to whatsisname?

I view the ever-spreading red
of her mouth through
the sides of my glass
and watch the night grow
long in the tooth.

November Sabbath

Damp squeeb o a day;
November rowin the lest
wizened aipple in a mould,
steirin the smell
o chrysanthemum leaves.

Ayont the fruitless brammle
bush, heukit tae the dyke,
the ashen giz
o a spent bonfire.

In the neist field
the blades o the plou
are slicin the stibble,
fauldin the furrows.

The plouman leuks ahent
at the land turning
on its ain axle,
gulls girnin in his wake;
a feathered clood
skraichen.

He switches aff;
waits for
a twa-meenit silence.

Winter Comes Early

i.m. Gordon Stephen

He's dying and
there is no turning back.

Mountains shrivel
into bleak abstractions
Dalnashian;
the weather closes in.

I switch the radio on;
hear the old familiar song:
We've only just begun to live . . .

Snow comes like
the laying on of hands.

The wipers slur.
A semi-circle slips
from black to white
then back to black.

The landscape dwindles
into frozen air.

The A9 does a
disappearing act.

Winter Solstice 1999
The night of the biggest moon this century.

After the mysteries of snow,
the thaw crept in.
Haar shrunk the land
to pale abstractions.

Trees grew above the clouds:
the smoking burn
unleashed a solitary heron.

When dusk fell,
stars came out like static.

A giant moon
rose above the wood
then cut itself in two
with a string of darkened geese.

The creaking of their wings
was the sound of ice on the loch.

Moonshadows trailed in our wake,
past starry-eyed sheep
in the lunar-raked stubble.

Wind chimes stirring,
the front door opens –
neither of us wants to go in.

Drummond Hill

In this white world,
summit and sky

are interwoven.
We are cocooned

in weightlessness.
The land lies inert,

space curving in on itself.
Out of the corner

of nowhere,
a small wind rises,

stirring the silence.
The haar hesitates.

Slowly, shapes form,
trees reveal themselves.

Loch Tay unwraps
a faded watercolour.

We descend,
our cover blown.

Loch an Eilein

Here,
the quait is
bruckle as ice.

Syne
the grey-lag goose
cums wingan in
wi the furst
flauchter o snaw.

The land ligs
time-warpit.

He touches doun;
a grace note
on the stave
o winter.

19

Deer in Winter

Snow-scripted pylons
loop the Strath
in weighted
scribbles.

White-stemmed
telegraph poles,
knowing no parameters,
fade into infinity.

Bone-white mountains
knuckle down to size
under the pale lantern
of a rising moon.

Rooted in
pine-meshed shadow,
four deer freeze in
a momentary glimpse.

Craigowl

Craigowl couries ablow
the furst flauchter o snaw,
steel pylons pyntin
frostit fingirs tae the sky.

Corn stibble, fibre-optics
skinkle i the reid
o the risin sun. Leaves
glued tae the grun.

An arrowhead o geese
are girnin waefu echoes.
The wauch o winter's
i the wun.

Writing Letters During a Power-cut

February
was in its element.

Cold cracked
the gap
between
the window
and the written word,

melting snowflakes
leaked beaded curtains
down
winter-tinted glass.

Water furled
from
a fractured spout:
metronomed
onto a zinc
pail.

Words faded
in the shade
of an unlit lamp.

Still Life

A row of dead crows strung up
between the telegraph wires.
A pigeon explodes like a pillow
and a fox cub stiffens in the ditch.

He's hanging up his gun;
getting rid of the place,
moving into town. He takes stock.
One collie, surplus to requirements.

But he didn't dig deep enough.
The vixen came in the night and
worked by the light of a winter moon.
The wind slipped its leash

and the evidence rose to the surface
to torment him; fear in his throat,
a tangle of bones and matted fur
and teeth locked in an everlasting grin.

Maister an Dug

He comes stridin
doun the ferm track
like ane o his prize bulls.

His shilpit dug
jouks back and forrit,
weel awa fae the pynt
o the blackthorn.
He greets me wi a nod.
Ay, it's a braw day.
His vyce draps tae a whusper.
Like tae see ma weans?

He pairts the lang grass
anent the dyke
wi canny fingirs.

In a moss-lined howe,
a flister o wee paitricks
an nutmeg-spreckled shells
pale as mulk.

The collie jinks
a wheen ower close.

Ye doitit bitch. Get intae heel.

The tae o his buit
sheens lik a ripenin ploum.

On Dod Hill

Day
creaks in
on its hinges;
an empty February sky
and a hawk making
a space for itself.

The land is sharp
with frozen grass-blades.

On the hard edge
of the horizon,
the trig-point:
granite glitter
of cold quartz.

Haematite
bleeds red
in the rising sun.
The moor crackles
under
cellophane wraps.

Water Music

A watermark becomes a darkened frieze
below the gutter. All night long the rains
have played a rap across the sloping eaves.

A bell-rope spun from water pitches chimes
upon an upturned pail. *Arpeggio.*
The clothes-line reeling three sheets to the wind.

An overflowing spout has struck a chord
against a clotted drain. The first tulip
has broken ground and April laid down roots.

The trees are singing in an old man's voice:
rhythm and blues. A flock of starlings makes
notations on the phone wires then ring off.

Inishmore Dawn

This is Galway
yet the shore is spun
Donegal tweed.

Woven shadows
hap
Inishmore Island.

Low slung cloud
lifts from the land,
spinning
the raw edge
of the world to a
fringed
umber and indigo

then
in a split seam
of a second,
day switches itself on
with the suddenness
of sun.

Crossing to Gigha

We have left our prints
on a distant shore
frayed at the edges.

The gap
widens.

Gulls girn in
harsh vocables

where the Sound deepens
to a blue-green.

Foam churns
like buttermilk
in the wake
of the ferryboat.

The thrum of the engine
fades.
Diminuendo.

In the land beyond
the marram grass
summer is a
shapeless haze.

On the Coigach Peninsula

In the half-light
of this spare land,

I keep the silence
at arm's length.

A symposium
of Summer Isles
huddles in
an autumn sea.

Suilven and Stac Polly
shoulder a fine mist.

Whiles, Cul Beg
sticks out
a hard neck.

Ben More Coigach
slopes off
to the shore.

Canisp meditates,
head high
in the clouds.

The peninsula skulks
incognito.

I keep the silence
at arm's length.

North Uist

The dim horizon distances itself.
Evening shadows inch along the pier.
A washed-out sun is drowning in the west.
A boisterous wind is changing down a gear.

Evening shadows inch along the pier.
Peat smoke drifts into a darkening sky.
A boisterous wind is changing up a gear
and in the distance wheeling curlews cry.

Peat smoke drifts into a darkening sky.
Storm clouds race towards the Hebrides
and in the distance wheeling curlews cry.
A single-minded boat puts out to sea.

Storm clouds race towards the Hebrides
A washed-out sun is drowning in the west.
A single-minded boat puts out to sea –
the dim horizon distances itself.

Glen Esk

Broun, peaty bree
atween ma taes
swurls cauld as ice
fae snaw cled heichts.

Nae braith o wun
tae dill the soun
o watter wimplin
throu the wuid.

Aside this rock,
time scoured,
I think on whan
I wis a bairn,

feet i the burn.
Still simmer's day –
ah'm sweirt tae leave
this place.

Old Dornie

Dawn
and there is
a shower-curtain
drawn
over every window.

I wipe
a crescent
of condensation
from the glass
with the heel of my hand.

Rainclouds ebb
beyond the Minch
in soft syllables.

Isolated showers
of girning gulls
come in to land.

The ghost of a sheep
is close-cropping
the machair.

Tanera Beg and Tanera Mor
are faded images
hemstitched to the
horizon.

View from the Cottage Door

Balancing the morning
on the end of an oar,
salted in his own element,
Calum is walking
on water. Again.

He jumps nimbly
from canoe to motor-boat.

There is a small gargling
as the engine
clears its throat.

The vessel sidles up to
the jetty where
visitors are viewing
new horizons.

In Loch Carron
the seals gather
on the rocks in
anticipation:

*How many tourists
will we see today?*

In Tempera
inspired by Erik Hoffman's painting Communion Day

In Tempera . . .
The Hebrides . . .

strung out in pale
brushstrokes,

an uninhabited land,
but for the bairn.

She is pale as an island
happed in mist,

five bluebells
flowering from her fist

and the road to nowhere
puddled with rainwater.

Images
empty themselves,
heather and lichen on a
hard-shouldered headland.

Over the rim,
smell the ocean
salting its might.

A driverless
road-roller squats,
incongruous as a
prehistoric bird.

Where are the gulls,
the oyster-catcher,
the cormorant?

Gone,
the way of
the emigrant.

Tracing the Ancestors

She is looking for a different angle
on her grandfather's tales of the old country.

A loaded Pentax with telescopic lens;
black and white film for dramatic effect.

Through a chink in the drystane dyke,
she can hear a snell wind scouring

the emptiness of a Sutherland horizon.
Dark clouds are weeping over Strathnaver.

There is the rise and fall of troubled seas,
the long exposure of deserted shore.

The house of her ancestors is in her head.
She steps inside and knows this is the place.

Snakes & Ladders

The sun is a crimson counter
flipping its lid.

I'm on the top rung
and the hairless man
is on the bottom . . .

Ophidian-eyed,
he's foreign to these parts.

There's a dice between his teeth;
a tattooed viper
needling up his arm.

He takes one step nearer,
executes a bow. *Your move.*

The symbolism may be biblical.
Heaven or Hell
I'm reaching for the light;
the inexplicable.

Book at Bedtime

I open the *Collected Poems*
and from the outer space
of the fly-leaf a
meandering many-legged
spider
trickles down the page
and comes to a
full stop.

I ask myself
could this be
a direct descendant
of Bruce's spider,
jet-bead body
strung on hairpin legs?

I ease him
onto the white web
of a tissue,
sidle through the door
and
into a night
with stars in its eyes.

MacCaig
takes cover,
in his well-thumbed
dust jacket,
smiling his cynic's smile.

Dreampoet

in the corner of my bedroom
lies Roger

he scans
his way through
my dreams
creating poems for me

but enough
of this McGough
imustremember
to give him the chop
stop
him in midflow
drag him back to the
library
where the woman
with understanding smile
will say
fine
twenty pence please

National Poetry Day

It's National Poetry Day today
says the faceless man over the tannoy.
There will be readings on the first
and second floors of the Centre.

Christ! There's me on CCTV.
Drop the dead dactyl.

For my next appearance . . . I will
foot it up the down escalator,
jingle the turnstile at the ladies loo,
rap around the Wellgate clock,
lampoon the punters in their tracks.

It's not like that at all. I'm trying
my damnedest to remain invisible.

Measure the reaction.
Two deaf pensioners,
a few open-mouthed schoolkids
and me scanning the shoppers
for one interested face.
Heroic or what?

The glass doors tick, tick then cut.
I'm out, into the concrete poem
of the Hilltown.

We Kin Laffatit Noo

The lie-brurry
thats whurrit wiz
a poetry re
ding by
whitziz name

red uz
a six wurd poem
wi the
obligiturry
four letter wurd
thrownin
turdsanat
ken

right enuff
tellt uz
his languij
wiz disgraceful

red uz anither
that soondit like
a shoapin list

we dun
the wrang thing
snickert

shooda seeniz face
he sez
tipicil
thickiz shitn
a boatl
the lottaya

ah gee up
kenma
heed duzny
buttnupthi back
if ye dinny unnerstaun
jiss fuckaff
tellnyi
gawn
ootma road

Yersel an Masel
fae the auld Erse

If ye come ava
come anerly at nicht
an step quaitly
– dinna fleg me.
Ye'll fin the key
ablow the doorstane
an me bi masel
– dinna fleg me.

There's nae pot i the wey
nae stuil nor can
nor rope o strae
– naethin ava.
The dug is quait
an winnae say a word.
It's nae shame tae him:
ah've trained him weel.

Ma mither's asleep
an ma faither's priggin wi her
kissin her mou
an kissin her mou.
Isnae she chancy!

Hae peety on me
lyin here bi masel
i the feather bed.

The Road to Donegal

The night is young
and leather-jacketed.
There's talk of bombs.
My feelings are explosive.

I stop the car and wait.
The engine ticks with nerves.
Barbed wire fuses the gate
dividing North from South.

My mouth is dry. The guy
behind the check-point
nonchalantly asks me why
I've come. *Business or holiday?*

And, *Can I see your licence?*
His tongue is speaking
my language. I am
crossing his border.

O'Malley's to McDonald's

Any minute now she will backtrack
into the infinite memory
of cracked leather settees,
old stone jars, dusty books.

Everything will come alive.
A bodhran will be drumming,
a step-dancer tapping out the past.
But the red brick is not a trick

of the fluorescent light
nor an outline she will recognise.
There are the ghosts of old men
choking on their Guinness.

Her reflection is an extra
in the plate-glass window.
The *smell* of change. Burgers, hot dogs
and the viscera of congealed egg.

Last Supper

He boasted he'd a mistress down in Cork
and that his wife was in the dark
about his extra-marital affairs.

The day he hit a one-way street,
the lid was lifted. In the boot;
rakes of red roses, liqueur chocolates,
two bottles of Chateauneuf-du-Pape
and one melodeon with missing teeth.

A curlicue of tape coiled in his lap –
Van Morrison cut off mid-Coney-Island
right at the bit where he stopped
at Strangford Lough. His wife
was meditating on a good-going wake
until the life-support machine kicked in.

She felt she could have stuck a Guinness bottle
in the hole that was his head.
Picking over the bones of the beat-up Renault,
she spied the wedge of scalp jammed in the radio.

Flipside of the moon, she laid it out
in clingfilm like a rasher of best back,
stuck it in the cold heart of the fridge.
She thought this was a clever thing to do.
The surgeon tried to fit it in, but no.

So she checked out the dog
who was straining at the leash.
The smell of flesh had sent him barking mad.

A hound might be fooled into thinking
– boneless chicken. The perverse kick
as she watched him licking
all but the willow pattern from his dish.

Elegy for a Would-be Carpenter

The undertaker washing his hands
with invisible soap;
stroking the surface of the coffin lid
like a second skin and you are talked
into buying that misshapen slab
of dark mahogany.

You said you'd make a table that would be
a talking-point. Bizarre, we thought but
you were right into the still-life of the workshop,
thickening the lathe with stour, sanding,
planing, smoothing the edges, coarse as coconut.
For days the house inhaled the smell of resin.

That September morning you were shaving
when a sudden shift of mood
tempered the mirror, your reflection
ghosting through the vapour, back slumped
over the lavatory seat.
Outside the sodium lamp had dimmed its halo.

Splintered blue, the ambulance lights spun
across the morning's retina.
Oxygen-masked, you said you'd watched the world
settle, your mother's voice lapping at the edges
of your senses. Cradled in the canvas
of a stretcher, you were a child again.

Buried under a snow of sheets,
capillaries branching in a tree of life
above your head. Digital red. Bleep. Bleep.
Upriver from Ninewells, a dull sun set.
An autumn haar whitened its bones.
The city glittered in a cold sweat.

Look at you now, adept at DIY dialysis,
cracking thin jokes about your bloated self,
fenced in by bannisters you face the music.
Touch Me In The Morning. Barbara Streisand
fading like quicksilver from your CD player;
that coffee table crouches like a Jonah in the corner.

Halfway to Paradise

There are unsound shadows
on the landing.

Halfway between Coronary Care
and Renal Dialysis,

a worry of old women
in white winceyette.

Age stares fish-eyed
at the floor,

fretting at her lifeline.
An amber puddle marks the spot

where inhibitions
have unstitched themselves.

Wheelchairs waiting in a row.
The porters' jokes bounce

rhetoric off the walls.
The lift doors open

to an unresponsive
Going Down.

A Shakespearean Actor Bows Out

My Granny swore she had the second sight.
The night the lodger took his life
she said she'd known that something strange
was going on. She'd had a warning.
That morning the pig hot-water bottle
had flown like a bird from her bed
and landed on
the far side of the room.

It was an omen.

All it took was two bob in the meter.
Later, when they'd broken down the door,
they found the actor
wasn't putting on an act any more.
Dead.

She said *What did I tell you?*
then for good measure, in a shaky voice,
When the spirit moves him, he will rise.

I slept in the attic and was on nodding terms
with the skeletons in her cupboards.
Mothballs rattled like pan-drops
in the jaws of the wardrobe drawer.
My hair was static electricity,
with the ghost of Coriolanus
performing nightly at the leaded window.

Afterwards when she offered me the pig,
I took
   cold
      feet.

The Diagnosis
For Ian

He's been tellt
he has nae future.
Ye switch aff;

listen tae the
soun o the engine,
tickin tae a stop.

Hark at the houlet
i the wuid,
wyvin a waefu sang,

a lang drawn-oot O.
Nicht is turnin
on a sternie.

See the siller sickle
o a laid-back mune
lichtin the land.

The end rig is in sicht,
the quernstane atween
winter an spring.

In the Sheltered House

Sometimes the light will catch you unawares
in the feedback from a liver-spotted mirror.

Seeing, not believing that the years
have made their mark. Acting the child, my mother

weighs up the possibilities.
Study the lifeline incised on your palm.

Where does it lead? How well I recognise
the signs. The times you've said that no-one cares.

Your pulse is dancing out of kilter. Quick
quick slow; a tablet underneath your tongue.

Don't look back. A gently closing door
is casting ill-defined shadows. Don't stir.

Let the tea-leaves settle in your cup.
Feet up, you read today's obituaries.

October

I see my anxious face
in endless shop windows
my mother stuck to my arm
like a burr

Looking back
a child-size shadow
is gaining

I wonder if she
recognises me

All she says is

*Ay, the nichts
are fair drawin in*

The Spirit of Christmas

He looks as if he's waiting for something:
'Eastenders' or 'Game for a Laugh',
with German subtitles perhaps?
Tightlipped now, deaf to the rain rapping
on stained glass or the landlord knocking
once the bank account ran dry.

He's tuned to virtual reality,
hunkered by the television set,
in the stour of a Weimaraner-coloured chair.
The TV listings journal's in his lap,
still open at the nicotine-tinged page,
dated 5th December '93.

Frost wrinkles its nose up at the window
and the heating has long since switched off.
The neighbours talked like empty corridors.
I can't remember when I saw him last,
someone said he'd gone off to a home.

The undertakers have been notified.
They will hook the tissue of a bluebottle
from the socket where an eye has been:
case him from the hardness of his chair,
break some bones in order that he fits
into a kist. The block of flats
in some forgotten corner of the town
will settle down to anonymity.

God knows the reason why the fairy lights
on his Christmas tree flashed steadily
for five whole years, stabbing sharp as ice.

Motor Neurone

A blue tractor unloads
sepia herring-bone prints.

A crimson sun tilts
over newly ploughed furrows.

Day walks in with a
spring in its step.

One lark in the sky.

Clouds tacking,
sheets flapping
and the land
laid out to dry.

I thought of him,
dragging his legs:
hyacinth blues
fraying the edge
of his senses,

him, mumbling
impossibilities . . .

*Days like this
make you glad to be alive.*

View from the Kitchen Window

I draw the curtains,
stare at my cold
reflections.

February frosts the land,
tilts the horizon to

an infinite white zero.

Two pheasants share
the drystane dyke.

Their exclamations mark
another
winter morning.

Two days hard frost;
the puddle's double glazed
and, on the path,
your footprints
gauge your going.

For My Son

The afternoon was
wheat coloured.

Time caught up
and carried you off.

You waved.

My smile was
put on and wide
as any new horizon

but when you turned
from me
an umbilical cord
broke its moorings.

I bottled up the tears
and rinsed them out
after you'd gone.

We share
the same moon,
the same stars,
yet we are
oceans apart.

Raw Round the Edges

She was on her knees
under the sink
trying to scrub the memory
of him away.

She found the cat's dish
with a faint freckling
of dun-coloured 'Whiskas'
glued to the edges.

The smell of it ran
right up her nose. She rose,
smoothed the plastic of her apron
over bruised legs

and as the bin shut its teeth
on the flawed dish,
she spotted the fermenting demijohn;
the dregs of summer wine.

The Day I Got New Sandshune

Saft-shaein up the
wrang stair, I raxed
for the haunle
an lat masel in.

Ma bearins had gaen,
somewey atween
the first an
third flair.

Fear pu'd me forrit
tho I kent the lobby
had cheenged
its spots.

It wisnae ma Gran's
aiple-pie smell but
byled cabbage an the mochie odour
o washin steamin roun the fire.

Twa wally-dugs grinned
at me fae the mantlepiece.

The auld wifie
picked up her shewin;
broke a threid atween
shairpened teeth.

The grandfaither knock
wis alive wi tickin.

The auld mannie
creaked fae the laither
o his weenged armchair,
an speired in a shooglie vyce

Whit's yer name then?

A door snapped shut
at ma heels.

Blowing Bubbles

The soap is smooth
as polished amber
in my hand.

Faint sepia scents.
Yesterday's child
is dipping a wire noose
in a tall tin
and blowing.

A bubble, hung
by a weighted
water-thread,
breaks loose.

The colours
of the rainbow
cut and run.
We watch together;
a spectrum of a cloud
with us reflecting
on a floating sphere.

And then,
the bubble bursts,
leaving the damp stain
of memory.

Red

A child aged four
a Mansion Polish tin,
razor-sharp around
the edges.

The sun slatted in
pale corrugations
through venetian blinds.

I was helping my Granny
polish the linoleum
surround when I knelt
on the lid.

It is still visible,
the white seam where
the pink stitches hold
my knee together.

Wash Day Sonnet

A'm keekin throu a telescope the wrang
wey roun. The washin-hoose is wabbed wi steam;
ma mither in a peeny tied wi twine
has 'Sunlight' soap-suds stipplin her skin.
She fills an auld zinc bucket tae the lip
wi watter fae the well. She smells o bleach.
Ma faither's sarks are tethered tae the rope
wi wuiden pegs. The mangle haunle creaks.
A saft slurry o stairch anoints the linens.
Fae in ablow the byler lid, the fent
miasma o moth-baas an steepin woollens.
Fragmentit images growe indistinct:
a windae hauds her sheddae in its frame,
her distant simmers spun wi daisy-chains.

G I Bride

The images are salted in her head,
a cardboard suitcase, passport, £10 note,
two copies of her birth certificate,
hand-sewn underwear in parachute silk.

A young girl jitterbugging up the gangplank
in Rita Hayworth curls and Persianelle coat –
the band plays *California Here I Come*
then *Auld Lang Syne*. Ships siren. Gulls girning.

Her father's tears. She'd never seen him cry.
Her mother's sigh. *You've made your bed* . . .
Chums wave home-made flags; their voices fading –
the water widening between them.

Old Photographs

The West Port turns into a silent movie,
the photographer a faceless executioner.
A disjointed voice from under a black hood
says *Watch the birdie.*

We're round a chair with barley-sugar legs.
My father stiff as starch in navy suit;
his tie an unaccustomed noose.
My mother in an eau-de-nil silk blouse
and turban, à la mode,
one hand exposed to show a wedding ring.

And me, myopic in wire-rimmed specs,
I feel the roughness of that tweed coat yet;
the rabbit fur stroking my neck.
The picture is the colour of dried blood.
The camera can't lie. It did.

My father's blackened face and hands,
mother on her knees scrubbing the stairs,
my brothers' faces glued with candy floss and
my sister's sights on America.

After the War

The parting in his hair was sheer precision,
his ginger moustache standing to attention.
Remembrance Sunday. How could I forget?

My Uncle Henderson, larger than life,
held us spellbound with his escapades.
His ship torpedoed in the war, he said

Don't ever let them say the Med is warm.
We swam towards this ship – the two of us
and just as we were making headway

she altered course. My voice was hoarse with shouting.
All my mate could say was "Right. That's it",
opened his mouth and let the tide come in.

Portsmouth, he worked a flanker. Trade was brisk.
Forging rail tickets. *Any destination*
guaranteed. Perth or Dundee? Ten bob each.

Until his father met him at the station.
The man in blue serge punched the ticket, said
under his breath *Nou tell yer son tae stop*

thae bloody fakes. We'll let him aff. THIS time.
Civvy Street and he resumed his trade.
A painter – he was one for jokes.

His shop became the *Pent House*. In his van
you saw the road beneath the pitted floor.
My car? He said he could drive anything

and sheered off half the beech hedge as he went,
cross-hatched his country with an ancient tent
and lost his eyebrows to an angry Primus.

The Cenotaph. Slate-grey November day
we watched the war veterans on parade.
A row of medals quivered on his chest,

behind the lines; lame dogs following,
a dark red poppy pierced his buttonhole.
He gave a brazen wink as he marched past

the wee men on the Cooncil and their wives.
The image of him unreels in my head –
death came, falling from an old school roof.

Elliot Beach

The weekend supplement was marking time.
The Coronation, nineteen fifty three.
A toffee-apple taste like summer wine,
spilled from the centre page. A child like me
was looking back towards the shore. She wore
a ruched elastic swimming suit with halter
neck, a gingham ribbon in her hair.
A man behind who might have been my father,
Brylcreem-smooth and in the summer heat,
his eyes pale ambiguities. The beach
is crowded. Uncle Louis bares his feet
and etching sepia prints, wades out of reach.
Turning the page, the images disperse
and vanish on the tongue like candy-floss.

Uncle Dave Meets Dietrich

The remembered sensuality
when she introduced herself;
a look designed to melt.

When she felt for the contents
of her leopardskin bag,
he caught the glitter
of the diamante clasp.

Eyebrow pencil, raspberry lipstick,
matches, silver cigarette case.
Chanel No5 perfume and
a swizzle-stick for her champagne.

What he found unsettling
was her musical saw;
the high pitched keening,
sinister as an air-raid siren.

Marlene and her million-dollar legs.
Ah! Falling in love again;
the intimate scrawled signature
at the end of her last letter.

Demolition

The JCB performs another trick.
The tenement buckles at the knees;
a pack of cards.

Shards of anaglypta
whirl like ticker-tape along the street.
The windows spit out glass like broken teeth.

A fireplace crouches;
an empty mouth defying gravity.
A frieze of lilac flowers
droops at the hem of one remaining wall.

The Burgh Engineer has had his fill. He joins
the traffic tearing down the dotted lines
of the dual carriageway,
towards the emptiness his wife has left.

Multi-Storey

Is this whit they caa
bein upwardly mobile?
He, the sclimmin staur

wi laither jaicket,
studs skinklin i the licht's ee
rived fae its socket.

Syne me, feart aboot
whaur cheils like him fit intae
this constellation.

The door skreichs open
on oor anonymity.
We are decantit

intae a weird warld;
a lane land, whaur the waas shout
an ill-fremmit leid.

Dundee Day Tripper

The ither day
a tramcar cam
rummlin doun
the Nethergate
o ma memory.

It stoaped outside
the Greens Playhoose,
whaur an auld film
flickert backarties
in black an white.

Ootbye, a puckle
camsteerie cooncil chiels
got cairried awa wi themsels,
yoked up a Trojan cuddy
an ploud throu the Overgate.

Craws cowpit
fae the corbie stanes
an the auld toun
turnt tae stour,
happit harns in hodden grey.

The bummer gaed.
Words skellt fae
the mou o the *Courier* biggin;
fell on deif lugs.

At the terminus
ma lines got raivelt,
laivin ma thochts
hingin like the washin
on the plettie.

Crossing the Tay Bridge

A vast blue wash
from bridge to sky

and a solitary boat tugs
a glitter of fishscales,

the estuary, a map
with no boundaries.

Tayport whitens its bones
in a sea of haar.

Rust-red stalactites weld
themselves into a hard-edged echo.

Labourer Keeping Warm

Morning insinuates itself
in black and white,
light thin as tracing paper.

Hissing coals flare
into the still air of a winter sky.

Hunkered on an upturned drum
the labourer raises his hands
in a blessing to the flames.

Frigid tenements
turn their backs on him.

A solitary figure, he is
meditating on tomorrow.
Snow on the lines and a tunnel
ending in an ominous black zero.

Engine Driver – Retired

When the steam cleared
the images stuck in his head;
lights palpitating in the gloom
of the engine shed
and the silhouette of
The Forfarshire reeking like
an old man running out of puff.

Names reeled from his tongue;
Cox Brothers, Lochee,
Thos. Muir, Son & Paton,
Smith Hood & Company.
Goods waggons shunting,
a whistle blowing –
the sounds catch in his throat.

Nightwatchman

Night crackled with the violence of stars,
forbidden fruit behind the orchard walls,
apples in abundance, damsons, plums
and wasp-infested windfalls left to rot.

A notice brass-tacked to the gate. *Keep Out.*
The nightwatchman was
silently skulking in the shed, stewed tea
thickening like tar on the blackened brazier.

Nestle's Milk, smooth as a woman's silk
underwear. Food for the soul. Dream on.
A semi-naked Marilyn blows xxx
from the pages of the *Sunday Sport.*
There's a fuzz of tinnitus from the transistor.

Something was troubling him. He watched
and knew in turn that he was being watched.
Shadows crept like razor-blades,
cutting a path towards him through the trees.
And when the moon drilled through a cloud
it got him right between the eyes.

Closing Down Sale

She's drawn like a divining-rod to water,
face to the glass, feverish as a wasp
buzzing to be let in on the act.

The blinds are at a tantalising level.
Down on her hunkers squinting up the legs
of Spice-Girl lookalikes with hollow heads,

she feels that giddiness which comes
with blowing money she can ill afford.
Hugging the weight of a fake-fur coat,

she recalls the bargain Louis Vuitton bag,
secreted in its vulgar shades of brown,
in a wardrobe whose doors cannot be shut.

Handbagging

Hands like a magician's;
make things disappear
into the thin air
of an outsize snakeskin bag.

Turkish Delight
and the aftertaste of guilt
sweeten her tongue.

Then she's out
into a vague September sun,
the wind frisking her pockets
in a street that can't remember
where it's at.

The Wardrobe of Paranoia

It's night-time in the wardrobe. Step inside.
Adjust your eyes to the row of shirts
dreaming themselves alive.

If you are scared of the dark,
this is not the place for you.
Take a knife. A sharp one.

There will be a black hole facing you.
Ignore the feeling of disorientation
and let yourself go.

Surrender yourself to the improbable.
Valium will lighten your fall,
before you hit rock bottom.

The mirror on the door will bring you back
to life. You'll barely recognise yourself,
convinced you're fatter than you were before.

The Face Factory

They caught her
on the vain side of the moon.
With little persuasion,
she let them stitch her up.

Rubber-gloved fingers
coaxed the needle through
unforgiving flesh until her skin
was stretched, tight as a condom.

She struggled to open her eyes
to a day tasting of anaesthetic.
Musak by Mozart,
dispensed like sugar-coated pills.

The blood-letting over,
she saw in the unflawed mirror
her youth looking back
over an old shoulder.

Face to Face with the Sixties

A slender image worrying the mirror;
kohl-rimmed eyes focus on a
Mary Quant haircut and skintight mini,
stiletto heels pockmark the lino.
Evening in Paris.

John, Paul, George, Ringo
She loves you, yeah, yeah, yeah. Lulu's *Shout.*
Breasts cone in a foam-lined bra,
laughter lines she couldn't edit out.
Pause for breath.

She thinks the past is done to death
and lights her umpteenth cigarette,
contemplates tomorrow; the unimaginable.
She'd have a tattoo on her upper arm,
a gold ring through a wizened nipple

and a nose stud for the hell of it.
Such frippery. Upstage the neighbours,
stop the gossips in their tracks.
Bingo. All the sixes. Sixty-six.
Growing old is just a bitch.

Last Tango with Magritte

My dancing partner's head is webbed in gauze,
His voice is mummified, his eye unseeing.

The picture haunts – I cannot put a face
to him. His mouth is dumb with folded linen.

The space between us shrinks gossamer fine.
The city-slicker in a sombre suit

has laid himself between my silken lines.
The gibbet spins; a tightening in his throat.

He's over-ripe, I peel his mask away.
The kiss of death is tasting how he feels.

Blue-bottle sounds of distant summer days
are coiling round the room. I take my meal.

Biographical Note

Born and educated in Arbroath, Lydia Robb lives in the Angus countryside which is a source of inspiration for much of her writing. Wife, mother, grandmother, she has been writing as long as she can remember but started taking her writing more seriously once the family had flown the nest.

Poetry and prose are widely published including in, *Chapman*, two *BBC* anthologies and both National Museum of Scotland anthologies, *Present Poets*.

Recipient of many literary prizes including winner of the Scottish International Open Poetry competition UK section, 1999, shortlisted for the Macallan/ *Scotland-on-Sunday* short story competition, 1998. Past winner of both the Robert McLellan & Hugh MacDiarmid silver tassies in the Scots. Language Society annual competition and first prize in the 1997 *Northwords* competition. She was awarded a Scottish Arts Council Writer's bursary in 1998.

Co-writer of *Grundstane*, an acclaimed outdoor drama performed in July 2000 at the Signal Tower Museum in Arbroath for Angus Council's Millennium project. Author of a one-act play *The Deil's Awa* concerning the illicit whisky trade in old Angus. This play is to be performed in and around the Angus Glens early 2001 and published in *Seven Angus Dramas* May 2001.

Her children's poems are included in an anthology by Constable & Robinson, entitled *Hilariously Funny Verse*, published late 2000. Involved in the compilation of *Caa Doon the Mune*, an anthology of modern writing in Scots for school children.